Gray As a Dolphin
Gris como un delfín

written by **Molly Dingles**

illustrated by **Walter Velez**

dingles & company New Jersey

First printing

PUBLISHED BY dingles&company

P.O. Box 508 • Sea Girt, New Jersey • 08750
WEBSITE: www.dingles.com • E-MAIL: info@dingles.com

Library of Congress Catalog Card No.: 2004092986
ISBN: 1-891997-58-0

Printed in the United States of America

●

ART DIRECTED & DESIGNED BY Barbie Lambert
ART ASSISTANT Erin Collity

ENGLISH EDITED BY Andrea Curley
SPANISH TEXT EDITED BY John Page

EDUCATION CONSULTANT Kathleen P. Miller

PREPRESS BY Pixel Graphics, Inc.

For Nikkiann

Molly Dingles

is the author of *Jinka Jinka Jelly Bean* and *Little Lee Lee's Birthday Bang*. As Judy Zocchi, she has written the *Paulie & Sasha* series. She is a writer and lyricist who holds a bachelor's degree in fine arts/theater from Mount Saint Mary's College and a master's degree in educational theater from New York University. She lives in Manasquan, New Jersey, with her husband, David.

Walter Velez

was born in New York. He attended the High School of Art and Design and later the School of Visual Arts. He has done illustration work for many major book and gaming companies. He is known for the popular series *Thieves World* as well as the *Myth* series for Ace Books. He has also produced trading cards for *Goosebumps* and *Dune*. In addition, Walter has illustrated several *Star Wars* books for Random House. He lives in Queens, New York, with his wife, Kriti, and daughter, Kassandra.

The Community of Color series is more than just a series of books about colors. The series demonstrates how individual people, places, and things combine to form a community. It allows children to view the world in segments and then experience the wonderment and value of the community as a whole.

Gray as a dolphin

Gris como un delfín

Gray clouds in the sky

Nubes grises
en el cielo

Gray as a whale

Gris como una ballena

Gray pigeons fly

Palomas grises vuelan

Gray as a rooftop

Gris como un tejado

Gray bucket for bait

Cubo gris para carnada

Gray as a shark

Gris como un tiburón

Gray exit gate

Puerta gris de salida

Gray as an otter

Gris como una nutria

Gray family of eels

Familia de anguilas grises

Gray as a rat

Gris como una rata

Gray silly seals

Focas absurdas grises

The color Gray is all around.

El color Gris está en todas partes.

Where at this aquarium can Gray be found?

¿En dónde en este acuario se puede encontrar el color Gris?

ABOUT COLOR

Use the Community of Color series to teach your child to identify the most basic colors and to help him or her relate these colors to objects in the real world. ASK:

- What color is this book about?
- Can you name the gray things at this aquarium?
- Can you find a gray animal in this picture?
- What gray fish are in this picture?

ABOUT COMMUNITY

Use the Community of Color series to teach your child how he or she is an important part of the community. Explain to your child what a community is.

- A community is a place where people live, work, and play together.
- Your family is a community.
- Your school is a community.
- Your neighborhood is a community.
- The world is one big community.

Everyone plays an important part in making a community work - moms, dads, boys, girls, police officers, firefighters, teachers, mail carriers, garbage collectors, store clerks, and even animals are all important parts of a community. Use these questions to FURTHER the conversation:

- How are the people at this aquarium interacting with one another?
- How are the people different from one another? How are they the same?
- What do they have in common?
- How is the community you see in this book like your community? How is it different?
- Describe your community.

ABOUT FEELINGS

Colors can describe as well as evoke different emotions. Encourage your child to describe the feelings that the color gray inspires.

- How does the color gray make you feel?
- Name your favorite gray thing in this book. Why is it your favorite?
- Name your favorite gray thing at home. Why is it your favorite?
- Can you tell how the people in the picture feel by looking at their faces? Do you ever feel the same way? When? Why?

TRY SOMETHING NEW... Dive in! With an adult, go to an aquarium and learn more about sea life. Find out what you can do to help keep our oceans clean.

community of color series